GIYA KANCHELI

NIGHT PRAYERS
from *Life Without Christmas*

for String Quartet

(full score)

ED-3928

First printing: July 1994

G. SCHIRMER, Inc.

DISTRIBUTED BY

HAL•LEONARD
CORPORATION
7777 W. BLUEMOUND RD. P.O. BOX 13819 MILWAUKEE, WI 53213

Born in Tbilisi, Soviet Georgia in 1935, Giya Kancheli studied composition with Professor Ion Tuskia at the Tbilisi Conservatory. As a student, Kancheli was among the leaders of the young Soviet avante-garde. After graduating from the Tbilisi Conservatory in 1963, Kancheli went on to serve for twenty years as Music Director of the Rustaveli Theatre in Tbilisi.

In recent years Kancheli has gained recognition as one of his country's most influential and well-known composers. Kancheli's scores, which draw inspiration from Georgian folklore, are filled with haunting aural images, varied colors and textures, sharp contrasts, and shattering climaxes. Perhaps best known for his orchestral works, Kancheli received the USSR State Prize in 1976 for his *Fourth Symphony*.

Of his music, Kancheli writes:

"When composing I never think of using specific means of expression. I establish basic themes, a dramaturgical scheme of the whole, and then gradually, note by note, create a musical progression. This progression should soar in the listener's imagination. It should convey the sensations of beauty and eternity streaming in the height of light. Above all, it should inspire the widely understood feeling of religiousness that is manifest in all the music dearest to my heart."

Night Prayers is the fourth part of a four-part cycle of independent chamber pieces called *Life Without Christmas*. *Night Prayers* is Kancheli's first work for the Kronos Quartet and was commissioned by the Beigler Trust and Lincoln Center for the Performing Arts. The Kronos Quartet has recorded the work for Elektra/Nonesuch (due for release in late 1994).

Duration: ca. 25 minutes

Premiere performance: March 14, 1992, Mozart Saal Konzerthaus, Vienna
U.S. Premiere: April 25, 1992, Alice Tully Hall, New York City
Both premieres were given by the Kronos Quartet

to the Kronos Quartet

NIGHT PRAYERS
from *Life Without Christmas*

Giya Kancheli

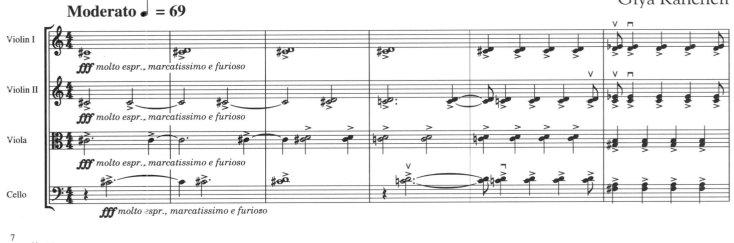

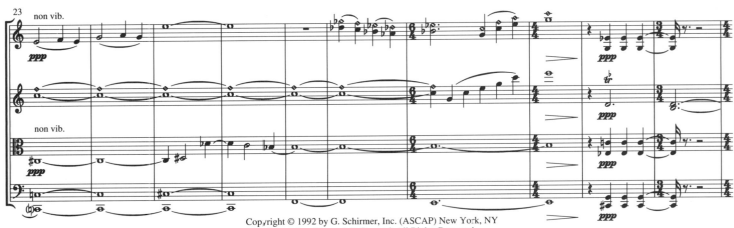

Con fuoco

Poco tranquillo

Lamentoso

Prestissimo

A tempo

* Do not synchronize with Violin I.
** Do not synchronize with the Violins.

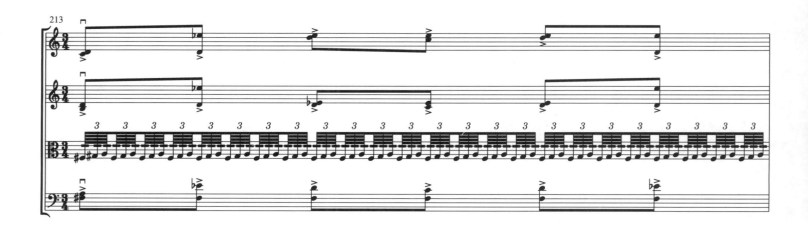

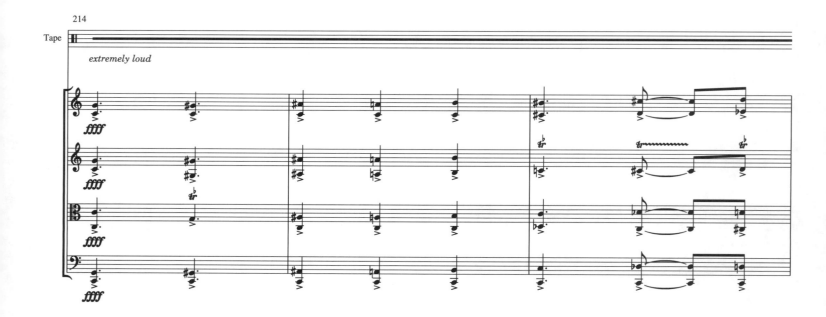

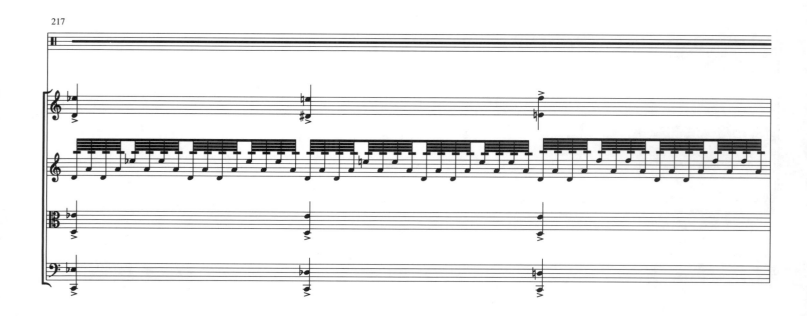

218

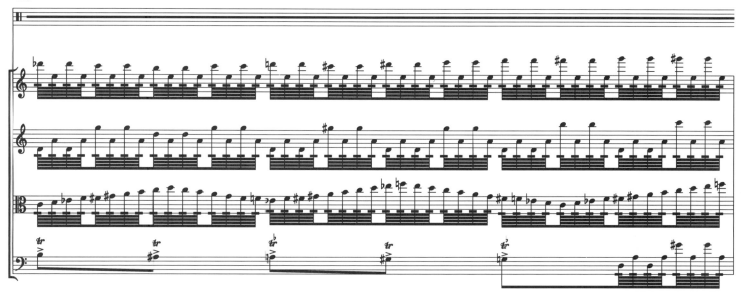

219

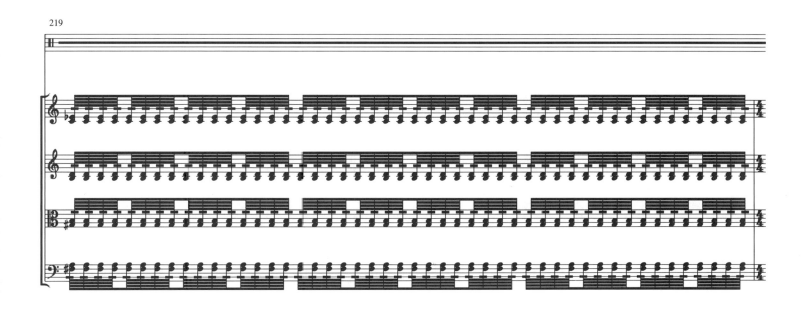

220

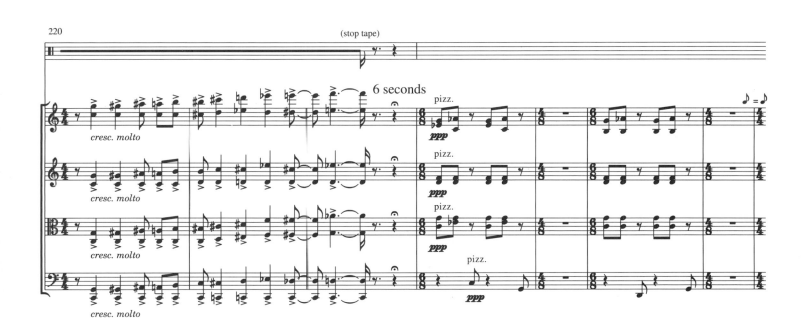

Poco meno mosso